*Faith, Love, and
the Joy of Living*

Faith, Love, and the Joy of Living

John J. Sidebotham

VANTAGE PRESS
New York

Cover design by Susan Thomas

FIRST EDITION

All rights reserved, including the right of reproduction in whole or in part in any form.

Copyright © 2008 by John J. Sidebotham

Published by Vantage Press, Inc.
419 Park Ave. South, New York, NY 10016

Manufactured in the United States of America
ISBN: 978-0-533-15843-0

Library of Congress Catalog Card No.: 2007904715

0 9 8 7 6 5 4 3 2 1

To my wife, Mary, and our five children, John, Peggy, Jim, Mike, and Tom who have made my life such a joy

Contents

Preface — xi

Words of Faith
A Flash of Light	3
A Gift from God	4
A Glass of Water	5
My Prayer	6
A New Day (Advent)	7
A Tapestry to the Lord	8
A Question, An Answer	9
Bless This House	10
"Come Home"	11
Creation/Salvation	13
God Bless You	15
God's Love	16
God's Mercy	17
I Am, The Babe of Bethlehem	18
I Came A-crawling	20
In God We Trust	21
"Jesus," I Said	23
Jesus Said	24
Oh Lord Hear My Cry	25
Open Up My Heart to Sing	26
Parable	27
Parable 1981	29
Parable 1991	30

Sunshine for Today	31
Tears	32
The Face of God	34
The Five Senses	36
The Message and The Messenger	38
The Peace of Love	40
The Calla Lily	41
The Easter Lily	42
The Empty Tomb	43
Touched by His Hand	44
Who Am I?	45

Patriotic Words

A Ballad of Archie Sherard	49
I Never Thought I'd See This Day (WWII)	51
July, The Month of Pride	53
Landing Ship Tank, LST 5 (Large Slow Target)	54

Words of Life and Living

An Old Friend	59
Cub Scouts and My Ego	60
Have a Nice Trip	61
Jeffrey's Skin	62
Logic of a Three-Year-Old	63
My Home Town	64
October	65
Oh Great and Hallowed Hall	66
Raking Leaves	68
St. Patrick's Pot of Gold	69
The Beauty of the Storm	70
This Old House	72
Weather Forecast	74
White Snow, White Clouds	75

The Coming of Spring	76
The Days of November	77
The Lizard Ladder	78

Words of Love

A Star Was Born	83
I Dare to Say	84
Goodnight My Love	85
Holding Hands with Mary	86
Profile of a Mother	88
Ring the Bell	89
Solomon's Wish	91
Time with My Love	92
To Lose You	93
To My Mother and Father	94
To My Wife	95
To My Wife at Childbirth	96
Three Loves Have I	98

Words for Weddings

A Wedding Prayer	101
A Mountain Spring	102
Love Conquers All	103
Our Wedding Prayer	104
Glossary	105
Three Kernels of Rice	106

Preface

This book is a collection of original poems and incidents, expressing my Faith in God, Faith and Love for our Country, and the love for my wife, Mary. These are personal moments expressing my faith, love, joy, and sober thoughts. They are about life, love, weddings, raising our children and working in the garden. All of these poems and thoughts come from the heart.

Mary has been my right hand, editor, and advisor for all of my words.

Thank you for reading this book. I hope you enjoy reading it as much as I have enjoyed writing it.

*Faith, Love, and
the Joy of Living*

Words of Faith

A Flash of Light

In the night of all this darkness,
A pause in the brightness of the sun,
From a small corner of outer space,
A flash of light is seen.

In the silence of all this noise,
In the calm of all this bustle,
Amidst the thunder of clanging cymbals,
A small clear voice can be heard.

He speaks to me out of chaos,
His words of comfort never cease,
To find a shelter, a haven,
My soul dreams of quiet and peace.

No longer is there trouble and sorrow,
By his hand and voice I am healed,
Through Him my salvation is assured,
The Father's Love through His Son, revealed.

Pay not attention to the chaos,
Let not the hustle and bustle preoccupy,
Focus on the light of His Countenance,
Christ Jesus our Savior is passing by.

Amen

A Gift from God

This gift has been from the beginning,
This gift will last till "Judgment Day."
This gift, no one dare keep it,
They must always give it away.

This gift is more precious than diamonds,
Often given to the poorest to share,
Yet may slip away from the richest,
And given to those who care.

This gift is not judged by its beauty,
Nor counted like ounces of gold,
But eases the burden of sorrow,
And fills the world with joy untold.

This gift is given by the aged,
The young, the weak and the new,
And brightens each lonesome pathway,
Refreshing as the morning dew.

This gift cannot be traded for silver,
Or kept unused for a day,
But must be shared each moment,
With those along the way.

This gift we give to each other,
Was sent from heaven above,
This gift we give and receive this day,
This Gift from God is "The Gift of Love."

Amen

A Glass of Water

The objects in this dream are, a black ink cartridge,
A glass of water and a white blanket.
I was trying to replace a black ink cartridge in the office printer.
As I was handling it I spilled ink all over the place.
There were gallons of black ink all over the floor.
What a mess. Everyone blamed it on me.

While trying to clean it up, all I received was scorn and ridicule.
No one would listen to my side of the story.
I used a white blanket to help soak up the ink and
When I was finished cleaning up the ink the blanket was still white.

As I stood before those who ridiculed me,
I had a glass of water in my hand and I told them,
Since you will not listen to me, like this glass of water,
I will pour you down the drain and you will ridicule me no more.

My Prayer

Lord, we are that water in that glass,
Lord, we want to be part of your plan,
Do not pour us down the drain.

Lord, in the beginning you made all things,
The air, the earth, the sky and the waters,
Lord, you hold all the waters in your hand,
Do not pour us down the drain.

Use us to refresh others,
Put us to good use that we may spread your word,
To serve you in newness of life.
Do not pour us down the drain.

In the waters of the Jordan, Lord, you were baptized,
You baptized us with water and The Holy Spirit,
You are the living water,
Do not pour us down the drain.

Lord, soak up all our sins with your blanket.
Cleanse the black ink from our lives.
Like the words of the psalm,
Wash me and I shall be whiter than snow.

Help us Lord to realize that,
We are the water in that glass,
Hold us in your hand.
Do not pour us down the drain.

Amen

A New Day (Advent)

The meadow lark is singing as the robin hops by,
And a soft clear light gently covers the sky.
The doe softly stirs while her fawn nestles warm,
And the stars dim their glow to make way for the morn.

The wise old owl softly closes his eyes,
And the opossum rambles homeward before the sun rises high.
The dew on the grass glistens brightly like diamonds,
And the air breathes of freshness no fragrance can surpass.

Now The Lord whispers softly as I lay on my bed,
"Come see what surprises for you lay ahead."
I have prepared a new sunrise, which has never been seen,
And flowers of such beauty, a garland for a queen.

"Today will be a glad day with a new Friend at your side,
Extend Him a welcome as you join Him in stride.
I am sending my Son Jesus to show you my love,
The Savior of All Mankind descends from above."

The glory of your Maker is forever in view,
And His word is saying, "It was made just for you"
Now rise from your slumber and greet each new day,
Lord Jesus awaits you, A light to show you the way.

Amen

A Tapestry to the Lord

Today we have a special and unusual prayer.
Today we want to create a tapestry,

A tapestry showing the glory of your creation.
A tapestry showing the glory of your resurrection.

We are like spools of thread lined up on a rack,
We are of different colors, sizes and texture.

We may be made of silk, cotton, wool or hemp,
Bind us together to reflect your glory and honor.

As the potter shapes and molds the clay to create the vase,
Weave us on the loom of your grace and mercy.

Use us as threads in a tapestry of your Church,
That we may give praise and glory to your Holy Name
Bind us together with your word
Weave us together in your service,
In Jesus' name we pray.

Amen

A Question, An Answer

Lord I have a question.
Please give me the answer,
Lord, I am perplexed.
Tell me what I should do.
Lord I have searched your words for an answer.
Please answer my prayer.
Lord I have a problem!
Where is the answer I seek?
The answer "I" seek?

Lord, you are the answer.
I am the problem.

Amen

Bless This House

Bless this house, Oh God we pray,
Bless this food upon the tray.

Bless the folks, who dwell herein,
Keep them safe from the power of sin.

Raise your hand to heal the sick,
Comfort the widow, bless the poor.

Make wise the foolish, Comfort all who mourn,
Cleanse our hearts with thy pure love.

Be our guide to heaven above,
In Jesus' Name we pray,

Amen

"Come Home"

My body now at rest, it lays. My days of toil are o'er.
I am now in the hands of my Lord. My fear of death no more.

My journey through this earth has ended, A new life has just begun.
My soul now lives in harmony, My Lord has said, "Come Home."

No one should ever say how sad, For now I live in joy.
Each day was filled with memories, of friendships that time cannot destroy.

My partner in this world of toil, She was to me a word of love,
Her voice was music to my ears. Like the cooing of the turtledove.

Each day we found a blessing, Each day a moment for mirth.
Each day was filled with happiness, Forgiveness and rebirth.

The Lord has blest us with His Love, His children we have raised.
To nurture, feed and love, To read His word and give Him praise.

Don't grieve my friends, But share this day of peace and joy.
For on this day I heard these words,
The Lord has said, "Come Home."

Amen.

Creation/Salvation

Beyond the hills of yesteryear, beyond the mountains of time,
No love was ever created, no greater love than Thine.

Before the sea of silence; before the coming of sound,
Your voice came out from the deep; your voice heard all around.

Below the seas of the waters; above the vast unknown skies,
Your voice was loudly saying; be patient, you will be my own.

Behind the curtain of mist; before there was solid ground,
Your love for man was forming; your plans will have no bounds.

A light was made from darkness; your plans for life were real,
Creation had taken its first step; your hand at the potter's wheel.

Your trust in man to live there and keep your creation true,
Has been at times unnerving; when sin made the air turn blue.

Salvation has been very costly, to send your son to the cross,
Where man reviled with such hatred; seeing not the chasm they had crossed.

We now all stand in judgment; for sin has entered everyone,
Grant us thy mercy and forgiveness and give us faith in Your Son.

For in Your great love, You have called us,
And through Your Dear Son, You have saved us.

Amen

God Bless You

God bless you in the day time,
And bless you in the night.
God bless you in the morning,
When the sun is shining bright.

God bless you while you work,
God bless you while you play.
God shield you when the north wind blows.
For His rain makes the flowers grow.

God bless you as you sleep,
And bless you when you dream,
God bless you when you stub your toe,
Or jump the widest stream.

God bless you when you are hungry.
Give thanks for the food you eat.
For God is the giver of all good things,
His love, His kindness and quiet sleep.

For He is there beside you,
To bless you as you weep,
For He is our Good Shepherd,
And we are His sheep.

Amen

God's Love

God's Love still blooms in August,
No matter how hot the day,
The fruit is showing its color,
Harvest is on the way.

God's love still blossom like the flowers,
The green fields filled with grass,
His love is ever before you,
And brightens the path over which you pass.

His love adorns every mountain,
Every shadow replaced with His light,
His love will calm every storm,
That shows its wrath in the night.

His love reflects peace and comfort,
That the Lord will provide,
For He now stands beside you,
Trust Him as your guide.

We will be kind to one another,
With a spirit upright.
And be true to each other,
As God keeps us in sight.

The prayers that we offer,
Our love for you we confess,
May God smile on each one of you,
And fill you with happiness.

Amen

God's Mercy

God has shown Mercy on me,
Should I not show mercy to others?

God has shown us love through His Son Jesus Christ,
Should I not show love to my brother?

God has provided me with his word,
Should I not pass it on to others?

God has shown me the light,
Now I must show others that same light.

God through Jesus Christ has forgiven me of my sins,
Surely I must do no less of my neighbor.

God has healed me,
Surely I must thank him, for all healing is divine.

God provides my daily bread,
Dare I not share it with my brother?

If I do not know how to serve others,
How will I know how to serve my Lord?

Lord Jesus, we ask for your help,
To serve others, to spread your word,
And to show mercy in the,
Name of Jesus Christ, Our Lord.

Amen

I Am, The Babe of Bethlehem

In Exodus 3:14 God said to Moses,
"I am who I am," tell them "I am" sent you.
"I am" and "The Babe of Bethlehem."
(The one and the same)

God's Love was in the beginning,
God's Love joined my Mother and Father.
"I am, The Babe of Bethlehem."

I was conceived in love,
I was nurtured with love.
"I am, The Babe of Bethlehem,"

My first day in this world was filled with joy,
Prayers that were said were words of praise.
"I am, The Babe of Bethlehem"

The shepherds in the fields were filled awe,
The angels sang with songs of glad tidings,
"I am, The Babe of Bethlehem"

My first visitors were filled with adoration,
The gifts they gave were offered in thanksgiving,
"I am, The Babe of Bethlehem"

The first sounds I heard were words of love.
My words to you this day are words of love.
"I am, The Babe of Bethlehem"

My Love to you this day is from The Father,
Rejoice this Christmas Day, upon My Birth.
"I am who I am,"
"I am, The Babe of Bethlehem."

Amen

I Came A-crawling

I came a-crawling, on my knees,
To find my Savior, to set me free.
I came a walking, side by side,
With Christ my Savior at the morning tide.

I came a-running, to my Lord,
To hear his word and speak his praise.
I came a-listening, for his voice,
His words have made this sad world rejoice.

I came a-speaking, His message to be heard,
To spread the word, in every hamlet, road and fjord.
I came a-singing to say what's in my heart,
To praise his name in song and verse, cymbal and harp.

I came here to Good Shepherd, to be with His Flock,
His Love surrounds us, Solid as a rock.
I came flying, on wings of faith,
It's Heaven I'm bound, where I'll be safe.

We come now with Thanksgiving, giving praises,
Honor, and Glory to our Savior evermore.
Fifty years may be small in the eyes of perfection,
But our hearts overflow with God's Love and Affection.

Amen

In God We Trust

"In God we trust" is ancient,
"In God we trust" is new,
"In God we trust" is eternal,
For the word of God is true.

King David sang of God's great glory,
Oh God, My Rock and Redeemer,
In God's name did he place his trust,
And blessedness was his reward.

Though Daniel was deep in the lion's den,
The wild beasts on every side.
God's word to him, "Do not fear but trust,"
In God's safety did he abide.

The words from a Cross on Calvary,
Our Lord Jesus cried out to say,
"Into thy hands do I trust my spirit"
Though pain and sorrow was his way.

In God's trust so sailed Columbus,
His words in the night, "Sail On"
Sail on to a land of promise and freedom,
That all nations might respond.

The pilgrims landed on a rocky shore,
A land so raw and bare,
Soon the land of milk and honey,
With plenty for all to share.

At Valley Forge on a cold winter's night,
With lips so cold, on bended knee,
Was heard the voice in a battle cry,
"Oh Lord we trust in Thee."

"Westward Ho" was the settler's cry,
With arms out stretched, His Bible at his side,
Before him lay vast deserts and prairies,
Before him stood the Great Divide.

From the longest hour at Corregidor,
To Iwo Jima's jubilant cry,
The souls of men respond to His call,
To trust, to rise, to die.

This land is our great heritage,
We live in a land brave and free,
So speak these words as you live each day,
"Oh God we do Trust in Thee."

Amen

"Jesus," I Said

"I am hungry" and He fed me.
"I am sad" and He comforted me.
"I am slipping" and He upheld me.
"I am cold" and He gave me warmth.
"I am lost" and He showed me the way.
"I am afraid" and He gave me courage.
"I have not life" and He gave of himself.
"I am alone" and He gave me flesh of my flesh.
I said, "Jesus, I will praise thee"
And He gave me wisdom.
I will sing of your name,
And all heaven resounds.
I said, "Jesus, we are happy
For you have bestowed on us your Love."
Thank you, Lord Jesus.

Amen

Jesus Said

"These are whom I see."
Do you see them with me?
Do you know them as I know them?
Do you know joy and not bless others?

Do you know thirst and not give others to drink?
Do you know the sick and not show compassion?
Do you see the blind and not show them my light?
Do you know the hungry and not share your bread?

Do you search for righteousness and not show justice?
I made you in my image, what I see you must see also.
When you hear a cry, comfort their tears.
When the blind approach, show them my light.

When you see hunger, feed them from your hand.
When you see suffering, show a compassionate heart.
When you show mercy I will sing and be glad.

"Your very body and souls must"
"Pray with me"
"Suffer with me"
"Comfort with me"
"Rejoice with me"
"Live for me"
"Die with me"
"And rise again with me."

Oh Lord Hear My Cry

In the middle of the night, Do I cry unto thee, Oh Lord
My faltering feet stumble over rocks.
Thistles tear at my arms and legs
Thorns fester and can not be removed.

My eyes burn with pain,
While searching with flickering candles.
My hands are full of blisters,
Tearing away vines that cling onto me.

My body is sore and bruised from evil pitfalls,
My mind is in torment as I follow false paths.
The nights are cold and the days are without sun.
Life without you, Oh Lord, I am lost in the mist.

Dear Lord, Forgive me of my sins against thee.
And against my neighbor.
I pray thee Lord,
Keep Thy Light ever before me.

Lead me in the paths of righteousness
That I may know Thy truth and feel Thy Love,

Amen

Open Up My Heart to Sing

Let me sing praises from my heart.
Fill my heart with songs of love,

Songs about your love for me.
The voice only sings what is in the mind,

Let my mind sing what is in my heart.
Let me sing praises to thy name,

Let me sing to thy glory and honor.
Let your voice be heard across the land,

Open my ears to listen.
Open my heart to sing.

Parable
(October, 1971)

The Lutheran Church of the Good Shepherd

Behold a pebble at my very feet,
To ponder o'er with eye discreet,
To kick or stomp to one's delight,
Or sail across the sky in flight.

This pebble, I gaze, there upon the ground,
Was made before my time was found.
Its presence here I know not why,
For God made the pebble when He fashioned the sky.

It could make a big splash if cast in a pool,
But the waves are soon gone, there remains but a fool.
This pebble has been fashioned by the Master who shares,
His love, His kindness, His Son, ours to share.

This pebble is precious for it bears His Son's name,
Where the sheep know The Good Shepherd when He calls them by name.
Twenty years has this pebble stood nigh on this ground,
Our task being to polish, to file and to sand.

His word is the polish that we handle with care,
The rough spots are soon gone and the cracks are not there.

As we polish and grind with reverent care,
The glory of our Lord must be reflected in there.

What a beautiful gem that we hold in our hands,
For God is the owner and gives this command.

Go forth to all nations, sing aloud His Great name,
Give God all the Glory and the pebble will remain.

Amen

Parable 1981
(The Lutheran Church of The Good Shepherd)

The year of grace now stands at thirty,
A gem in the palm of His Hand.
Blessings and kindness overflowing,
To people all over the land.

Our task has not diminished,
The harvest is still in the field.
Our mission remains,
To teach, to reach and to tend.

The days now past show His Glory,
His suffering, His Love and His Compassion.
The days ahead reveal His Promise,
A vision of growth, faith and devotion.

Come listen to the voice of the Good Shepherd,
Come pick up his staff in your hand.
Come stand in the light of His countenance,
Make His wish your command.

Amen

Parable 1991
(The Lutheran Church of The Good Shepherd)

Forty years has been but a moment,
Forty years has been but a day,
Forty years filled with blessings,
An abundant outpouring of love.

Forty years of faith in our Savior,
As we look toward the morrow.
The seeds have been sown,
The green plants are showing.

The flowers are starting to bud,
It's up with the dawn to the field.
The harvest is ready,
The need for workers is real.

I still hear the young children crying,
The aged still moan, all alone,
The widow mourns with her grief,
The hungry still empty and cold.

My Lord gives me faith in His word.
My cup is overflowing with His love,
My faith still needs to grow,
Awake my soul, Awake.

Amen

Sunshine for Today

As we took our places in church,
The day was cloudy and gloomy,

I remarked to my wife that we could sit here,
As the sun usually does not shine on this pew.

A few minutes later as we sat in prayer,
The sun shone through and
The Lord seemed to say,

"No matter where you sit in My Church
My Son (Sun) will always shine on you."

Amen

Washington Irving wrote these words:
"There is a sacredness in tears.
They are not the mark of weakness
But of power, they speak more eloquently
Than ten thousand tongues.
They are the messengers of overwhelming grief,
Of deep contrition, and of unspeakable love."

My thoughts for Easter.

Tears

Tears of joy, tears of sorrow,
Tears of love, Tears for tomorrow,
Tears of laughter, Tears of woe,
Tears that hide, and Tears that show.

If a child doesn't get its way,
Tears often flow like rain,
As a man there have been tears of sorrow,
And a few tears of pain.

Today! These are tears of joy,
These are tears of joy for Christ my Savior.
I thank God for the Tears shed on Calvary,
Because they were tears shed for you and for me.
I can see the Tears of joy shed by all the Angels,
When Jesus returned to heaven,
I would say there were a great many starry eyes,
On that First Great Easter Day.

They say you must have a human body to shed a tear,
But one of the greatest joys will be to shed a tear in
Thanksgiving and
In praise for my Lord Jesus Christ
When I meet him face to face.

I feel close to Him when a tear appears,
It's as if a veil comes over my eyes,
And His voice is saying,
"Be still and know that I am near."

Amen

The Face of God

I have seen the Face of God and now I must die.
I have seen The Face of God and He is majestic,
I have seen Him in the mountains,
I have seen Him in the oceans,
I see Him in all of His creations.

I have seen The Face of God and He is Awesome,
His Face is in the lightning and thunder,
His Face is in the mighty river.
I have seen The Face of God in His love for you and me.

I have seen The Face of God and He is kind and gentle,
His Face is in the beauty of the flowers,
I feel His Hand in the gentle wind,
And in the gentle flow of a mountain spring.

I have seen The Face of God,
In His Redeeming Son Jesus Christ,
Who is my Lord and Savior.
He is hope where there is despair,
He is Faith when I am lost.

I see The Face of God in the first strains of the organ,
His voice is heard as the hand bells are ringing,
And as the choirs sing forth their melodious anthems.
I have seen The Face of God as His Word is proclaimed.
His Face is seen in the Waters of Baptism.
I have seen Him on the Empty Cross.

I have seen The Face of God and now *I* must surely die.
I must die unto my own self righteousness.
I must die to all worldly possessions and temptations.

I have seen The Face of God,
And now *I* must die and live only unto Him,
For He is Jesus Christ my Savior.

Amen

The Five Senses

The Five Basic senses,
Taste,
Touch,
Hearing,
Sight,
and Smell,
Each sense requires a response,
Pleasant or unpleasant,
Acceptance or rejection.

Each sense is alive.
Each sense has meaning.
Each sense creates an image
Each sense requires a decision.

Today we ask,
To taste of your abundant bounty
To reach out and touch with someone with a helping hand.

To hear your word.
To see you in all your glory.
To smell the fragrance of your presence.

You have also given us two other abilities,
The ability to appreciate and,
The ability to love.

Help us this day to appreciate what you did for us on the cross,
To love one another as you have loved us,
Giving glory and honor to your creation.

In Jesus' name we pray.

Amen

The Message and The Messenger

Peace be with the messenger. The message has been delivered.
The voice crying in the wilderness, Has been heard throughout the land.

The messenger, faithful in his task, To hear the message is all that we ask.
Each day he had a story to tell, Each day he served his Master well.

A helping hand, a comforting word, A candle light in the dark of night.
He was there to hold my hand, To push back the dark and show God's light.

His voice was clear and forceful, His words of scripture were hard to ignore,
His words of love, comfort and joy, Will live in our hearts forever more.

We have a friend in common, "Jesus Christ" whom we all hold so dear.
Each day has been a blessing, To know that He is near.

Your partner through these many years, A wife, standing at your side,
To encourage and to comfort you, And join you in your daily stride.

The day has come to set aside, To recognize the Psalms you've raised,
Pastor Ron and Marilyn, We sing to you our songs of praise.

God Bless Both of You.

Amen

The Peace of Love

The peace of love shall be my cape,
Thy grace and mercy shall cover my face.

I shall not want nor weep no more,
Where joy will be forever more.

My guilt of sin in life was driven,
My sins, through Christ, have been forgiven.

Each day I seek to know him better,
Each night I sleep in quiet slumber.

With eternal life in heaven above.
Heaven for me will be thy love,

Thy loving arms to hold me tight,
To sleep in peace throughout the night.

No longer shall I need to roam,
Thy dwelling place shall be my home.

Amen

The Calla Lily

The Calla Lily, Its color so white
Lifting its face to the light.

A flower now blooming in the season of Lent,
To the glory of God, this flower has been sent.

Lent, the season of spring, the season of hope,
The season to reflect, to prepare the way of the Lord.

Hold out your hand; come to Him while He is near,
With your hand in His, you have nothing to fear.

The Easter Lily

The Easter Lily, shown in white perfection.
To show your Love, each flower blooms in all directions.

The stem shows a sign of a struggle, still a flower of perfection.
On a Cross, His Son, made to suffer for our Salvation.

This flower now faces all of us, saying. "I died for you."
Look at the Cross, See God's Glory,
Go now and tell His story.

The Empty Tomb

Lord, we solemnly reflect on your death,
The empty tomb is hard to understand,
But we rejoice in Your Resurrection
For you are leading us to the Promised Land,

The lilies, the mountains and valleys,
All nature is of your creation,
The rivers and lake reflect your Glory,
Truly now is a time for celebration.

As the lilies break forth to show God's glory,
Your Holy Word we now proclaim,
Help us to serve You,
To the Glory of Your Holy Name.

Amen

Touched by His Hand

When you touched my hand, You touched my heart.
As you touched my heart, You touched my soul.

When you touched my soul, You made me whole.
When you made me whole. I told my neighbor.

When I told my neighbor, He told his friend.
When his friend told me, I was felt truly blessed,

Touch my hand again Lord,
That the whole world will know of your love.

Amen

Who Am I?

LBW page 121–24 (Baptismal)
Pastor said during my Baptism,
"John, you are now a Child of God."

Who am I to sing praises to my Lord? "You are a child of God."
Who am I to worship my Lord? "You are a child of God."
Who am I to receive his blessing? "You are a child of God."
Who am I that you should love me? "You are a child of God."
Who am I to serve you? "You are a child of God."
Who am I to die and Live again with thee?
"You are a child of God."

How may I worship thee?
"Confess that you are a child of God,
I will send the Holy Spirit, Trust me."

How may I sing praises to your name.
"Confess that you are a child of God.
I will send the Holy Spirit. Trust me."

How may I serve others?
"Confess that you are a child of God,
I will send the Holy Spirit. Trust me."

How may I bless others?
"Confess that you are a child of God,
I will send the Holy Spirit. Trust me."

How may I know that I am saved?
"I have sent my son Jesus to die for you,
Confess to him that you are a child of God,
I have already taken care of the rest. Believe Me."

Amen

Patriotic Words

A Ballad of Archie Sherard

What ever happened to Archie Sherard?
His name remembered, on this day in the fall,
His name ringing clear as a bell in the night,
A soldier, who had answered his country's call.

His mother, so happy when he came home,
His deeds in life were all so real,
His battle scars were hard to see.
Returning to life, now, a chaotic ordeal.

No one knew of the horror he'd known,
The nights of terror and days of hell,
His mind and body now in torment,
His soul, pealing like a tolling bell.

The lives he saved, in peril of his own,
Others had seen his deeds of honor,
His hands, reaching out,
To save a friend, in all that horror.

He had lived next door, but saw me naught,
Life for him, all but gone, so it seems,
His life, now shredded, like the threads of time.
For him, life was just a horrible dream.

Each day he reached out to find his way,
Reaching high, on the walls of the quay.
Losing all strength with each rising swell,
What man will save him from this labyrinth of hell?

His name, we remember, His deeds we applaud,
This man, of high regard, whom we did not save,
Bless the name of Archie Sherard,
Bless the name of Archie Sherard.

Amen

I Never Thought I'd See This Day (WWII)

It was a day so long ago.
Our hearts were young and strong,
Our spirits wild and free,
It was a day of uncertainty.

Each one had hope, kept under wraps,
Each one though longed for home.
Each knew not what the day might bring,
For the night was long and cold.

But in that day a bond was made,
A bond of love ad caring.
Unseen as each went on his way,
Today this bond, we are sharing.

The years have been good to all of us,
We've known some bitter times,
You each has kept within his heart,
A place for his early friends.

Each one remembers where and when,
Memories that will live forever,
A laugh, a cry, a helping hand,
Of drinks we had together.

Our fears we shared, the deaths we saw,
A friend that died, now resting at his Mother's side.
The memories may have faded but are never really gone,
The present is now, all around us as the future has just begun.
We thank God for watching over us, his blessings we all have received,
A land so dear to share our dreams, this country that we call our home.
As we join again in friendship, to drink again to those not here,
To keep alive their deeds of honor and bless those gathered here.

Amen

July, The Month of Pride

I'm proud to be an American,
Proud to be from Ireland,
Proud to be from Germany,
My blood I'll shed for thee.

I'm proud to be an American,
Proud to be from the Orient,
Or from the Middle East,
I bring the best that I can be.

I'm proud to be an American,
Proud to claim Africa as my roots,
Proud to serve where ever I can,
This land now I call my own.

I'm proud to be an American,
To give others the same freedom that I claim,
To live a life that makes you proud,
A land so free and richly endowed.

I'm proud to be an American,
Each day I stop and thank my God,
To sleep at night, unafraid of the dark,
To rise each day with hope in my heart.

I'm proud to be an American.
My heritage I proudly claim,
Her colors of her flag I daily display,
This land I love is home for me.

Landing Ship Tank, LST 5
(Large Slow Target)

I may not be the fastest ship, nor make a rising wake or frill,
My shape was open to ridicule, to maneuver took all my Captain's skill.

I may not be considered a fighting ship or known as a ship of the line
But my service and devotion to duty will live throughout all time.

No bowsprit to adorn my bow, no sails to unfurl and wave,
My crew relied upon God's word eternal Father, strong to save.

My hull was made for a purpose, I rolled with the rising sea.
My decks were as flat as a playing field my cargo made ready and free.

A simple task was all they asked, it was against all sailing lore,
Breach your bow upon the beach, put your cargo safe on shore.

I left my mark upon the sand and opened wide my doors,
The trucks and jeeps roared down my ramp,
Amid the battle din and raucous score.

On Anzio, Salerno, Normandy, Tinian, Guam, Saipan,
Wherever my cargo was put ashore.

We delivered where they said,
We delivered, then went back for more.

Time and seas have now erased, the bow prints are no more,
But the memories of that long ago will live in man's soul forevermore.
We were there to fill a purpose, a service rendered in time of need,
And now we live in memories, still, my crew has said, "Well done indeed."

Words of Life and Living

An Old Friend

Today I met an old friend,
I haven't heard from for years,
An old friend who lives in my memory,
He comes to me when I am sad.

He comes to me on wings of sound,
He comes to me with words of faith
He comes to me with sounds of love,
And even in the song of a dream.

He comes to me when I need him,
This old friend is a song,
An old friend who brings a smile,
I look for him every day.

Each note I hear is familiar to my ear.
Each song brings back a memory,
These words of love
Have a warm place in my heart.

May the songs you hear today,
Bring an old friend back into your heart,
And old friend who will make you happy,
Happy enough to make you smile.

Cub Scouts and My Ego

After having spent many years as a Boy Scout Leader,
I was privileged to be invited as,
The guest of honor at a dinner on Scout Sunday.

After dinner as my wife and I were seated,
At the head table;
I, in my uniform and neatly trimmed (white) beard.

Many of the Cub Scouts came up and,
Were asking questions which further enhanced my ego.
But one question was asked that I was not prepared to answer.
It really took the wind out of my sails.

One of the Cub Scouts asked in all sincerity,
"Sir, are you the one who started Scouting?"
Needless to say the beard came off soon after that.

Have a Nice Trip
(Dedicated to my black and blue eye)

The yellow line is there for a purpose,
Step up,
Step down,
It could even mean, uneven ground.

Two steps, One step,
Or no steps at all,
Disregard what it says,
And you're due for a fall.

But if you don't take notice,
And assume what's up is down,
You're bound to end up, (like me)
Lying flat on the ground.

Now pick yourself up,
Try to act nonchalant and tenace,
You've just scored a shiner,
And a black and blue face.

So listen to this experience,
Look twice as to where you are,
The next step you take,
You may be in for quite a jar.

Mary's really a nice gal,
She really didn't hit me.
The truth is,
The pavement came up and bit me.

Jeffrey's Skin

One day as Jeffrey was talking to his mother he said, "Mama, am I growing up? Am I getting big? My skin is feeling too tight for me. My fingers and toes feel like they are being pinched. And it's hard for me to run real fast. Every time I eat my tummy feels so full. And I like to rub up against the side of this log because my skin itches."

"Yes," Jeffrey's mother told him, "you are growing up but your skin doesn't expand like some of your friends. You have to shed your old skin as you grow up.

"You don't have to buy new clothes as you grow up as a new skin is right under your old skin and it will just be the right size for you. Many other reptiles like snakes also shed their skin as they are growing up."

The next day Jeffrey was so surprised when the skin on his nose began to slip back over his head, then he pulled his right front leg out, then his left front leg came out.

Pretty soon he had most of his body out.

"Hey!" said Jeffrey, "I'm feeling better already."

The skin slipped over the rest of his body, then his back legs came out, then his tail and he was able to walk right out and leave his old skin lying right there on the ground.

Jeffrey then went for a walk to showing off his new skin and saying to all his friends, "Look at my new skin. See how big I am."

Logic of a Three-Year-Old

Marcus (3) and I (Grandpa) were playing with his train set when Uncle Bill stopped by from work to change his clothes before playing golf.

As Bill went by, Marcus asked where Uncle Bill was going and I said, "To the bathroom." Marcus then asked if he was going to the potty and I said, "No, he was going to change his clothes," which then brought up the next most logical question, "Did Uncle Bill wet his pants?"

My Home Town

A place to live, to call your own,
To live your life where you are known.
The city where everyone walks in style,
Where all the neighbors take time to smile.

With hearts and hands and love to share,
Helping hands will always be there.
Where the law of the land is born and declared,
The voice of the people, all thoughts are shared.

Sacramento Solons were my favorite team,
At Edmonds Field, they were my dream.
River Cats and Kings now take reign,
The Monarchs too on their way to fame.

Sacramento, born of silver and of gold,
Great riches to be mined, to have and to hold.
A railway hub, and a port of call,
A welcome sign, good business for all.

Where trees and gardens adorn all the streets,
From jazz to the classics, where good friends meet.
The harvest is plenty, rich soil at our feet,
With fruits and veggies, and grapes that are sweet.

This town, Sacramento, that I hold so dear,
I call it "My Home Town" because my heart is here.

October

October, the tenth month of the year,
Octagon, an eight-sided object,
Octogenarian, a person between the ages of 80 and 90,
I am an Octogenarian.

This is the month for Octogenarians.
Why do we call ourselves the cream of the crop,
Because, like cream we always rise to the top.

The years 80 to 90 and the years in between,
Shows that life can be happy,
For I am a King and you are my Queen.

This is a month of beauty,
When everyone looks his or her best,
Inward beauty also means, our souls are at rest.

The years are filled with wisdom,
Each person knows the lessons of life,
Passing it on to the youngsters,
Hoping they will not endure any strife.

We know that forgiving is a part of living,
We forgive because we have been forgiven,
Our Lord Jesus was the first to say, "I forgive."

The month, October, we say hello to our neighbors,
Wishing them health, wealth and a long life,
Whether it's at work or at play,
As an octogenarian, I hope you have a nice day.

Oh Great and Hallowed Hall

Once stood here, a great and hallowed hall,
Its walls, once lined with flags unfurled,
Its banners held on high,
Now its flags are furled and left to die.

Once stood here, a noble knight so tall,
To pay homage, to show respect on this day.
Then bowed he, before his King and Queen,
His victories on the field to display.

Beneath the sky of heaven and on earth,
His deeds of honor he now regales.
A fair maiden saved, the dragon slain,
A kingdom saved from the northern gale.

Fair maidens surround the court in awe,
Each, eager, their charms to display,
Each hoping, his heart, they might thaw.
The voice of the knight to say "yea" or "nay."

The King, his sword raised in Honor,
The King adorned with Crown, Scepter and Chain,
I dub thee, Knight of The Royal Order,
A Day of Grace, I now proclaim.

A land of peace, all prisoners unchained.
A Royal King and Queen, truly ordained.
From God, from whom all Blessings flow,
From each subject, loyalty obtained.

Once stood, a staunch and hallowed hall,
The floors of marble, walls of alabaster white.
Its ceilings of radiant silver,
And golden lamp stands, their luster, bright.

Once stood here a Great and Noble Hall,
Through time, now no windows, no beams.
For noble and peasant alike,
We live now in this city, The City of Our Dreams.

Raking Leaves

Falling leaves are such a mess,
To rake them up, a chore no less.
Each day a few leaves will say, "I'm going to drop."
Others say, "We like this place high at the top."

Why don't they say, "Let's all drop together."
It would save me time and I could enjoy the weather.

Each day I rake a few, those near the door,
Next day I rake, then rake some more.

On the other hand I like their plight, the leaves on the willow,
As they change colors to red and yellow.

What a joy last summer, sitting beneath their shade,
The green leaves of spring above me,
In my hand, a glass of lemonade.

No matter what the reasons, whenever I complain,
Raking leaves is really a pleasure,
I enjoy their beauty and forget the pain.

So if there is a chore that must be done,
Look on the bright side,
Even a few leaves are better than none.

St. Patrick's Pot of Gold

Today is your lucky day,
We have a pot of gold to share.
Golden songs from everywhere.

The songs we sing are golden songs.
Each note is like a fleck of gold.
Each song then becomes a coin of gold.

Songs of the Irish, Songs of love,
Songs that make you all starry eyed.
Songs of humor and songs of pride.

This pot is filled with gold.
This pot is filled with golden songs
Golden songs for everyone.

Sit back, relax and enjoy today
As we sing for you,
A pot full of golden songs
Songs to fill your loving hearts.

The Beauty of the Storm

The Storm, not to be outdone
To show its awesome strength
Until its course has been run.

The lightning betrays the dark of night.
The thunder applauding with all its might.
The rain is saying, "Don't leave me out,"

I too have something to say, "Have no doubt."
As the waters rise and say, "make way,"
The banks of the river have little to say.

Every snowflake throwing its weight around,
Adorning every tree, making white the ground.
The waves in the ocean, (let every ship sound the alarm),

"I am in charge here,
Let no man think he can do me, harm."
Sailors riding out the storm, silently they pray,

Any port in a storm is the order of the day.
The wind blowing free over all the land,
Every leaf and tree, bends in homage to its hand.

At the end of the storm all is forgiven,
The flowers say "Thanks," the trees stand anew,
The air has been cleansed, a rainbow is seen,
The hills, now covered with grass that is green.

The snow covered mountain, saying with a smile,
"Look at my white crown I'll be wearing for awhile,"
Every ship puts out to sea, fair weather ahead,
Every sailor finding his way, every sunset is red.

The earth now adorned with colors galore,
Peace covers the land once more.
Now sit back and relax, it's a brand new morn
We have seen and felt,
The Beauty of The Storm.

This Old House

Dear Lord, this old house is creaking,
As the wind blows on a stormy night,
This old house is enduring the test of time,
As it waits for the coming of light.

This old house has seen the sunrise,
And all of your creations surrounding it.
This old house has been to the mountaintop,
And sailed across the seas abounding.

This old house has had many dreams,
And many of its dreams come true.
This old house has been a stopping place,
A shelter and home under a sky of blue.

This old house has felt the patter of little feet,
And heeded the sound of a crying child.
This old house has known the sounds of joy and laughter,
And knows the signs of children acting wild.

This old house has known its sadness.
And shed many a somber tear.
This old house has seen dear friends depart,
But faces the night without any fear.

This old house has experienced your love,
The strength of many friends I value.
This old house fears not destruction,
For this old house was built by you.

This old house built not on sand,
But built with the strength of your love.
This old house asks only for today.
As we listen to the cooing of the turtledove.

This old house has experienced neglect and decay,
Your hand has provided repair and restoration,
This old house once was lost,
Now through your grace it has received salvation.

This old house seeks your word in every moment,
Your words of love strengthen us in every way.
This old house now gives thanks to its Maker,
For we have received our grace for the day.

Weather Forecast

Stand by for the latest weather news,
Stand by for the latest Hot Flashes
It will be just one of those days (not unlike yesterday?).

Wait while I take off my coat. Please hand me my sweater?
Will some one please open the window? Please close that window.
Is it hot in here? I'm sweating. Who opened that door, I'm cold.

No it's not my imagination. Get out of my sight.
Who put all these blankets on the bed? Quit hogging all the covers.
I've got to shed some of these clothes. May I borrow a sweater?

Who turned up the thermostat? Who turned down the heat?
I don't understand it. Don't you understand?
No, not now. You don't love me any more.

Why is it so humid today? I'm breaking out in a cold sweat
No!! I'm not cranky, what makes you think I'm irritable?

Now for the latest weather forecast.
The coast is clear dear. I still love you.

Technical Adviser and Weather Forecaster
My Wife

White Snow, White Clouds
(30,000 feet above the mountains)

White snow like cobwebs, stretching out its tentacles,
White snow turning to light blue as it gathers rest.
White snow turning the earth into pools of emerald and gold.
A blanket of snow for a crown, A land so fair, to be so blessed.

White snow, resting, quiets, without strife.
White snow in the spring, reaching out in torrents,
White snow, creating rivers of life.
White snow carving its way to the sea.

White clouds drifting above, ready to descend,
White clouds hover softly watching the quiet scene below,
White clouds then whipped into a storm,
Shaking trees and flowers as they grow.

Silent pyramids of green all standing in a row,
The trees, all silent, their arms, many bare,
The shadows of life on the meadows below,
For life is their color, the ground they must share.

Man's footprints now show and his scars are many,
This mark, He has made, now a reason to stare,
For this beauty was made in God's name,
Does man not seem to care?

The Coming of Spring

April showers, they show nature's power,
After each rain, we see a new flower.
These flowers of beauty, now on display,
These flowers of beauty, are here to stay.

The Blue Bells are ringing,
The birds start their singing.
The Golden Poppies are now in full bloom,
California fields, providing the room.

The azaleas so red, the lilies so fair,
Each in its own way, we dare not compare.
The bees on their quest to gather the honey,
Then hurrying home, to complete their journey.

There's the garden to till,
Tomatoes to be planted, squash in every hill.
The trees attired in their blossoms of pink,
An act of reverence, noble and distinct.

Created by God in all His Glory,
Creating for us, this wonderful story.

The Days of November

November has it s days of gloom,
The sun is there, but it seldom shines,
As the storm clouds gather,
We wonder if it will ever shine.

The birds of the fields are headed south,
The squirrels are snuggled away in a burrow,
A place where they'll be warm,
Sound asleep, as they wait for tomorrow.

The harvest has been garnered,
The hay, put away in the barn,
Grandma has filled all the jars with jelly,
But Grandpa just spins another yarn.

It's time to take stock,
How full is the larder? the pantry? the silo?
Hay for the horses, silage for the cows,
For the chickens, there's a bin full of Milo.

We give thanks to the Lord for all his blessings
The crops have been harvested
Each day we give thanks for one another and
To Jesus Christ our Lord and Savior

Amen

The Lizard Ladder

Help! Help me, I've fallen into a hole. I can't get out. Won't someone come and help me get out? Oh please come and help me.

Jeffrey and his mother lived in Uncle John's back yard. He has a garden filled with all good things to eat; strawberries, tomatoes, carrots and beans. Jeffrey especially liked the bugs that came to eat the vegetables in Uncle John's garden.

Uncle John had left several brush piles near the garden just so Jeffrey and his Mother would have a place to live. Jeffrey lived in a brush pile that was filled with lots of leaves to help keep them warm in the winter. Each morning he would come out and sun himself on a large limb. It felt so good and he needed the morning sun to help warm his body.

One day Jeffrey went for a walk near the garden and went near a large fishpond next to Uncle John's tool shed. That's where Uncle John kept his tools that he used in the garden.

The fishpond was deep and the sides were very steep and his mother had told him not to go near the pond as he might fall in and even though he knew how to swim. His mother said it was not a very safe place for a lizard to play.

Now Jeffrey was a big lizard and he thought he could easily get out in case he did fall in. Many times he had stopped by for a drink or to watch the water flowing down over the rocks and it made the nicest sound and was a nice place to rest. Sometimes he caught some bugs that came near the pond.

It was one of his favorite places to spend a few minutes each day after he had been looking for some worms or bugs to eat. The fishpond had some plants growing near the edge and he liked to reach up in the leaves and catch his favorite bug or fly.

But today there was no water in the pond. Uncle John was cleaning the pool and had drained all the water out. It was empty and dry.

Uncle John had put all the fish in a bucket while he cleaned out the pond.

As Jeffrey climbed the plants he slipped and fell into the pond. Now Jeffrey thought, *how am I going to get out?* He ran all around the bottom but couldn't find a way to get out.

He cried out but no one heard him. He tried climbing the sides but there was nothing to hang onto. He ran all around looking for a place to climb up but he was trapped in the bottom of the pond.

The sun was shining bright now and he was getting quite warm. Jeffrey said, "Oh I hope someone comes soon as I am so hot.

"Oh, oh, I'm in trouble now, here comes a strange-looking creature and I don't know what to do. There is no place to hide. If only I had a way to climb up out of here. What I need is a ladder. Yes! That's what I need, I need a lizard ladder.

"Oh, I'm so scared."

"Now I know who that is, that is Uncle John and he has something in his hands. He has some nice big rocks and he's putting down in the bottom of the pond. Yes that's what he's doing, he's building me a ladder. He's building me a lizard ladder so I can get out.

"Now I can go back to his garden and help him grow some large ripe tomatoes."

As soon as Jeffrey got out, Uncle John started filling

the pond with nice clean water so the fish would have a nice clean pond to swim in.

Thank you, Uncle John.

Metaphor to The Lizard Ladder

We too have fallen from our Garden of Eden into the black hole of sin from which there is no escape on our own.

We too are calling for help to relieve our suffering and death.

Our cries have been heard and help has been provided in the Death and Resurrection of Jesus Christ our Lord and Savior.

A ladder has been provided for us to return to God through Faith in Jesus Christ where we too may enjoy the fruits of heaven.

Words of Love

A Star Was Born

A star was born this wonderful day,
To shine with radiance along the way,
A star was born this winter night,
To praise her Lord with all her might.

A star was born this December day,
To show God's love and lead the way.
A star was born this happy night
To guide her children in one true light.

A star was born. Her love does not tarry,
A star was born. Her name is Mary.

I Dare to Say

I dare to say, "I love you"
I dare to say, "I care"
I dare to say, "It's heaven"
This marriage that we share.
I dare to remember, "The past"
I dare to enjoy, "Today"
I dare to say, "Of the future"
It will be brighter than the past in every way.
I dare to say, "I'm happy"
To have you, "As a friend"
I dare to say, "I'll love you"
Through time that has no end.

Your Husband

Goodnight My Love

I long to be with "My Love"
My heart is always with "My Love"
"My Love," is always near,
"My Love" the one I hold so dear.

"My Love" slows down the howling wind,
"My Love" restrains the rising tide.
"My Love" fills all my days with light,
"My Love" holds back the dark of night.

Each day is blessed and made complete,
Each night we rest in harmony.
The music of her voice I hear,
With hands to wipe away my tears.

Her smile breaks through the darkness,
His presence, like the stout oak tree.
Her voice like that of the turtle dove,
Each night, we whisper "Goodnight, My Love."

Holding Hands with Mary

As a child it was;
"Hold me, mother," I need your love,
"Daddy," hold my hand so I won't fall,
Friends, holding hands as we play.

Then Love steps in; "Mary, may I hold your hand?"
A blush fills my face on our first date,
Hands across the table,
Your hands are so nice and warm.

Christ holding our hands as we become one.
Holding hands as we see our first born.
The hand gently rocking the cradle
The hand that raises a hurt child.

Holding hands as we climb the highest mountain.
From the depths of despair I reach for your hand,
I always look for your hand to keep me safe,
To know that you are near.

Holding hands means we are traveling together.
It means we are striving for the same objective.
Holding hands as we romp beside the sea,
As we stand at the crest of a hill, our hands entwined,

An extended hand is an extension of the heart,
A helping hand goes a long way.
Your helping hand is always there when I need you,
May we always be found "Holding hands."

As we hold hands on this our fiftieth year of marriage,
Our hearts beat as one.
Our hands and our lives join together in praise to God,
Lord, we pray that Your Hand will always be guiding our hands.

Profile of a Mother

Have you seen her smile?
It radiates of warmth and love.
Day after day, mile after mile.

Have you felt her love and affection?
Warm, exhilarating and freely given.
A bowl full of love, served up with a ladle.

Have you tasted her cooking?
God gave us taste buds just to appreciate her talent,
Apple pie, whipped cream, great for finger licking.

Have you seen her beauty?
Fair to behold among all that have seen her,
The Song of Solomon describes her to a tee.

Have you heard her voice in the middle of the night?
A voice of comfort that dispels all bad dreams,
Bringing comfort and sleep till the morning light.

Have you seen her stand in the middle of adversity?
Her family has no fear of the unknown.
To her adversary, she shows no pity.

Have you felt her demand for respect?
A boy at his mother's knee grows up to be a man.
Each child she bears knows what to expect.

All of us have had a Mother.
All of us have been blessed by God.
All of us have indeed seen an Angel from Heaven.

Ring the Bell

It is fall and school has started

Do you remember those days?
Do you remember "Miss Bell"
Our fourth grade teacher?
Our fourth grade teacher,
We loved so well.

With love and kindness,
Her classes she taught,
We loved every lesson,
In her charms I was caught.

Each day her smile sent me years ahead,
To my young eyes
She was so lovely to see,
I wonder if she will "wait for me"?

Her voice, like that of an angel,
When she said, "Johnny, come here,"
Could this be the time?
When she'll say, "She'll be mine."

One day a tall stranger came into her life,
He filled my heart with pain and strife.
He took my love and left me stranded
Like a little calf I was hurt and branded.

The years have passed, I'm grownup now,
But when ever I ring this bell,

(Ring the Bell)
I'm remember my fourth grade teacher,
Her name really was "Miss Bell."

Solomon's Wish

Though Solomon's wish was for wisdom,
And Samson had Delilah so fair,
My thanks for what God has given me,
Is far beyond compare.

Though Moses led all of God's people,
And Abraham had a tent to spare,
My life without your presence,
Would be fraught with sorrow and despair.

Now David's kingdom was mighty,
And Saul fought the mighty foe,
My love for you is as fervent,
As you stand like the grazing doe.

Now Job had a terrible affliction,
And suffered such horrible pain,
Your love is like sweet balm and fine lotion,
Pure and as gentle as light soft rain.

Now the many years of or marriage,
Is small compared to Methuselah so bold,
But your Love, your Kindness and Devotion
Outshines all these stories of old.

Time with My Love

You are my every second,
As the moments delightfully tick by.
You are my every moment,
As each hour fills the sky.

You are my ray of hope,
As each morning greets the sun.
You are my day complete,
You are my life and meaning.

Through every season and year eternally,
For without you time would not be.

Amen

To Lose You

If I were to lose you my eyes would cry
If I were to lose you, my heart would die.
If I were to lose you, could I no longer stand?
If I were to lose you to God's kind and gentle hand?

To My Mother and Father

God's Love was in the beginning,
God's Love joined my Mother and Father,
I was conceived "in love,"
I was nurtured "in love,"

My first day in this world was filled "with love,"
Prayers that were said this day were filled "with love,"
The first smile I received was filled "with love,"
The tender hands that held me were filled "with love,"

My first meal was filled "with love,"
The tears that were shed were "tears of love,"
The first words that reached my tender ears were filled
"with love,"
Love must be very important in this new life,
I think I'm going to enjoy it.

Your newborn son

To My Wife

Fifty Years of Love
Fifty years of dreams fulfilled,
Dreams, yes, more than life itself.

Fifty years of remembrances,
Filling our hearts with love.

Fifty years of happiness,
With never one day of regret.

Fifty years of work, heartbreak and accomplishment,
Fifty years to bear and raise our children,

Through which God has made us strong.
For fifty years you and I have had one true love,

Fifty years God has been there to pick up the pieces,
With a never ending supply of love.

With God's blessing we pray that,
Our love for each other will live forever.

Amen

To My Wife at Childbirth

My eyes are wet,
My throat is dry,
My lips give but a whisper.

I've never seen this scene before.
Oh my God, what have we done?
To show my love, Oh God
Did I create this pain?

As I stand at the foot of her bed,
My wife in such pain and joy,
Before my eyes a new life is born.
God is saying "You were made for this."

My son, so little, born into this world so big,
He knows that his life has changed.
A change of magnificent proportions,
So sudden and so bare.

His thoughts are: (I'm sure)
"Where am I? in this unknown world.
I long for the comfort of my mother womb.

"I'm lost, I'm lonely, I'm cold.
I'm in a world not of my choosing.
I cry out for love, I cry out for love."

My love for her grows deeper as I sense and feel her love.
For her child, and this man, who is standing in awe.
I know not the pain she bears.
I only know my love for her is reaching greater depths.

What love is this,
To bear this pain for me.
The love of agape, (you offered your life for me)
That I might live through our son.

The gift of life is from above.
Our thanks and praise to God,
For His love, His grace and His mercy.
From Whom all blessings flow.
Amen

Loving you more than ever,
Your Husband

Three Loves Have I

Three loves have I to cherish,
Mother, Wife, and Daughter fair.
A mother's love to bear me,
And guide me all her days,
A mother's love that shields me
And leads in a righteous way.

A wife whose love is warm and fervent,
Inspires me to grandeur above.
A love with ardent expression,
Yet tender like the wings of a dove.

The love of a daughter is most precious,
A gift pure as gold twice refined.
A love with inner most feelings
That commune with her father through time.

Three loves have I to cherish,
Mother, Wife, and Daughter fair.
Each love though different in meaning,
It is the voice of God, His love we all share.

Amen

Words for Weddings

A Wedding Prayer

God put all the stars in their orbit,
Their paths are far apart,
All creatures have their calling,
But to man He gave a heart.

You two must make a decision,
Your actions must be discreet,
You may search o'er the entire world,
To make your lives complete.

Each time you pray that someone is near,
To share your hopes and dreams,
For every heart to be complete,
It takes two to make a team.

God has brought you two together,
To share your lives with Him,
To live your lives in harmony,
With the love of Christ that never grows dim.

Each must give their heart to the other,
This is not a light endeavor,
For when you give your heart in love,
The bond you create will last forever.

Each song we sing, in thankfulness,
Each prayer we offer, in praise,
We ask God to bless you,
In this marriage you now engage.

Amen

A Mountain Spring

Your marriage will be like a mountain spring,
A fountain of fresh clean water,
An out-pouring of love that comes forth with joy.

Your marriage will be like a gently,
Flowing stream as you cherish one another,
To provide love and life in a whole new world.

Your marriage will be like a mighty river,
Flowing through valleys, dashing over rocks,
Creating magnificent water falls.

Your marriage will be like the ocean,
Touching many far off lands.
You will hear the pounding surf and,
Feel its soft caress on the shores that surround it.

Your marriage will be the source of new life,
An abundant life, Restless at times,
Yet with a purpose as it journeys to the sea.

We pray that your marriage will always be like,
"The Stream," "The River," "The Ocean,"
Always anxious to return as rain,
To replenish the earth with fresh clean water,

"For Your Very Own Mountain Spring."

Love Conquers All

Where the mountain meets the sky,
And the ocean greets the shore,
May your love be as intimate,
And glow as never before.

As the wave crashes on the rock,
And the thunder responds to the lightning,
May your love find such excitement,
And be never ending.

As the sun pushes back the darkness,
And its rays gently warms the earth,
May your love be one for the other,
Filled with happiness and mirth.

As the wind in the trees gently kisses the leaves,
And the sun glistens bright on the dew,
May your love be ever so gentle,
As you start life anew.

As the world turns to rest,
And night gently covers the sky,
May your love find peace and harmony,
As you speak and act in reply.

Against all the forces on earth,
May your love stand tall,
For God is sending His love,
And Love conquers all.

Our Wedding Prayer

This is a most Blessed and Happy Day
The Lord has said, "It's a Holy day"
This is a time, "You both declare"
This is a time, "You both must share"
This is a time, "You open your hearts"
This is a love, "Now set apart"
This love you give, "Is not in vain"
This life together, "God will ordain"
May your hearts now, "Beat as one"
May your love now, "Be well done"
May your love be, "One for the other"
May you care, "Each for the other"
May your happiness and joy, "Overflow"
May His smile on you, "Bestow"
God will, "Tend and nourish all"
God will answer, "When you call"
God will always be, "At your side"
In His love, "May you Abide"

Amen

Glossary

"Blessed"	Deeply concerned with God, with dignity and honor.
"Happy"	Being in and showing good spirits.
"Holy"	In the service of God.
"Declare"	To bring to public notice.
"Share"	To give out in equal portions.
"Open your hearts"	Available from a concentrated point.
"Set apart"	Firmly set away from all others.
"Is not in vain"	But with honesty and integrity.
"Ordain"	To set forth, expressly by God.
"As one"	The ultimate point to love.
"Well done"	In a considerate manner.
"One for the other"	Bright and clear.
"Each for the other"	Going beyond what is expected.
"Overflow"	An overwhelming flow.
"Bestow"	To give formally and officially.
"Tend and nourish"	To promote and sustain.
"When you call"	To go or to seek out.
"At your side"	One who labors with you.
"May you abide"	In His Grace and Mercy.

Amen

Three Kernels of Rice

The evening was quiet as we sat in the night,
Lit only by a candle, still, then suddenly bright.
Our world for a moment as we pause in the night,
Then rejoice, for the future holds joy and delight.

We stood at the altar when my heart took this vow,
"All my love I pledge to you now,"
There was laughter and tears and many Good-byes,
And a wish of "God bless you" from one of the guys.

Now the light brightly glitters, and there shown in your hair,
Three kernels of rice, a little girl threw there.
Now rice is the symbol of wishes so nice,
For purity, happiness and newness of life.

These are the blessings that we pray for his night,
A clean heart, your happiness and a life in God's sight.
May the Blessings of God in His wisdom unite,
Our marriage and lives in His Glorious sight.

Amen